Ray Allen: The inspiring Story of One of Basketball's Greatest Shooters

An Unauthorized Biography

By: Clayton Geoffreys

Table of Contents

Foreword

Before Stephen Curry, there was a man who caused so much fear from opposing defenses that they would start half court pressing him the second he passed midcourt. That man was Ray Allen. A legend in his own right, Ray Allen is one of the greatest shooters to ever play at the professional level. With a deadly fast release, Ray Allen was a lethal shooter for many elite NBA teams, most notably with the Boston Celtics when he played alongside Kevin Garnett, Paul Pierce, and Rajon Rondo. Few players have the uncanny ability of Ray to release the ball so quickly and with such precision. His contemporaries would only be the likes of Stephen Curry, Steve Nash, J.J. Redick, and Kyle Korver in raw ability to launch the three-ball. While many younger basketball fans may not remember Ray's earlier years, Allen was a star in his own right when he played for the Seattle Supersonics and Milwaukee Bucks. Thank you for purchasing *Ray Allen: The inspiring Story of One of Basketball's*

Greatest Shooters. In this unauthorized biography, we will learn Ray Allen's incredible life story and impact on the game of basketball. Hope you enjoy and if you do, please do not forget to leave a review!

Also, check out my website at claytongeoffreys.com to join my exclusive list where I let you know about my latest books. To thank you for your purchase, you can go to my site to download a free copy of *33 Life Lessons: Success Principles, Career Advice & Habits of Successful People*. In the book, you'll learn from some of the greatest thought leaders of different industries on what it takes to become successful and how to live a great life.

Cheers,

Clayton Geoffreys

Visit me at www.claytongeoffreys.com

Introduction

The three-point shot is the deadliest spot to score from in the whole NBA. It's a game-changer that could either bring the team back after being down by a lot or seal the game away as a dagger shot. It's the kind of shot you need to spend hours of work on and several days of repetition to master, or at least hit at a good clip. In the history of the NBA, a lot of games have been sealed or put away early because of the three-point shot. And in league history, nobody has ever hit more of those shots than the sniper they call Ray Allen.

With almost 3,000 career three-pointers made, Ray Allen is the finest outside marksman the league has ever seen from a historical standpoint. He was one of the few players that lived from the three-point arc as his mindset was always to shoot the ball from the outside as much as he could. But Allen did not do so just because he wanted to. Making a lot of three-pointers is not as simple as putting up a lot of attempts from that spot on the floor. But Ray-Ray did so because that was the skill he mastered from a young age. He's put hours of work and repetition to learn that shot, and he's mastered it at several spots on the floor to be effective from well all over outside or inside the perimeter.

But, to become the best three-point shooter in the NBA, mastering your shot is just one part of it. A lot of players in the history of the NBA have mastered the art of shooting the ball. Such players are Larry Bird, Dale Ellis, Glen Rice, Dell Curry, *Dražen Petrović*, and Mike Miller, among others. All of those guys have mastered the art of spotting and camping outside the three-point arc to shoot the shot they've perfected. But Ray Allen is more than just a spotter on the floor. He's also mastered the art of moving without the ball to effectively use screens or elude defenders using a lot of constant motion on the floor. This technique has given him tons of open looks and opportunities to shoot the three-pointer without a hand in his face.

Ray Allen, considering that he is in constant motion on the floor trying to look for screens or the best open spot, has also always been one of the best-conditioned players in the league. Stamina is key when it comes to being a great shooter because of how much movement it entails. Shooters always have to be well-conditioned at the tail end of close games so that their legs remain fresh and in top form for possible dagger shots to win the game. Allen has always kept his body and his conditioning in top shape, and that longevity is a part of his game that has helped him hit tons of three-pointers, even when he was past his prime.

With Ray Allen hitting three-pointers night in and night out and with him being one of the best gunners in NBA history, he has become a two-time NBA champion, a 10-time All-Star, and an All-NBA Team member twice. He's compiled a total of 2,973 made three-pointers in a span of 18 years, and he's also scored a total of 24,505 points in his career as an NBA player. As pure of a shooter as Allen was, he was anything but one-dimensional as he's scored 18.9 points on average in a career that was almost two decades long. The fact that Allen has played 18 years is amazing in itself already, and that's a pure testament to how well-conditioned he always was.

Because today's NBA game has been predicated on a lot of three-point shooting, a lot of shooters have been thriving with how the style of the league has changed. Shooters like Stephen Curry, Klay Thompson, Damian Lillard, Kyle

Korver, and James Harden have all been All-Stars primarily because of how well they shoot the ball and some, if not all, of those players, have worked on what Ray Allen has started. In fact, two or three names of those mentioned above may even have developed into better shooters than Allen, and we may see guys like Curry and Thompson breaking the record in made three-pointers. Nonetheless, though we may see Allen's record broken in a few years, it still does not change the fact that he was the best the NBA has ever had in a very long time, and he's held that spot for the longest span possible. We may not see him on the list of best shooters with how the league has been changing, but rest assured that Ray Allen is still one of the best at hitting the long ball, and has been since the league's inception.

Chapter 1: Childhood and Early Years

The great three-point shooter was born as Walter Ray Allen on July 20, 1975. Ray Allen was the middle child of five siblings parented by Walter and Flora Allen. Because Walter was a welding specialist working for the military, the Allen siblings lived their life bouncing between one military base to another. In Ray-Ray's case, he was born when the family was based at the Castle Air Force Base in California. Ray and the family would even spend time in European military bases like the Bentwaters Air Force Base in England. But most of his childhood was spent bouncing between bases in America, such as Edwards Air Force Base and the one in Altus, Oklahoma.

Jumping from base to base was how Ray Allen was first exposed to organized sports. His first sport was the great American classic called football. Football was the first sport that Ray-Ray played because of how available of a game it was for families living on military bases. All you need is a big field, and you already have a football match. Aside from football, Ray Allen could also play baseball as it was also a relatively easy sport to play when moving to different military bases. As a child, Ray Allen was a prominent Little League player and was even said to have been good enough to go pro one day. But, as we know, that was not the road he took to get to the life of a professional athlete.

Ray was not a particularly big child in his early years, and that physical aspect led him to play sports that do not necessarily require height. But when he turned 10, Ray Allen had a growth spurt that led to him to play a little more of basketball than any other sport. He first played that game when the family was stationed in the Edwards Base in California. Since California is a hotbed for basketball, Ray-Ray was able to join an organized league for young children. As his mother Flora pointed out, Ray Allen seemed like a natural for the sport of basketball, even in his first organized game.

When Ray Allen was 12 years old, he began working with a man named Phil Pleasant, who ran basketball leagues and camps in California. His associations aimed to keep young children more involved with sports in order to keep them away from the troubles of society. Working with Pleasant upped Allen's game to a whole new level. His offense and his fundamentals increased to levels unparalleled for a young Ray Allen. He was so good that, at one point when the family moved to the Shaw Air Base, his father was punished for insubordination for an incident that involved Ray-Ray. Walt took his son to play with other military fathers and sons but was told to take Ray out of the building because he was not old enough. But he did not let Ray-Ray leave in the belief that his son was bigger and better than all of the people in the gym on that day. Indeed, he was.

Chapter 2: High School Career

In 1990, Ray Allen entered Hillcrest High School located in South Carolina. He was 6'2" by then, and was both big and good enough to play for the varsity team as a guard. He was an instant impact player for Hillcrest and became one of the best players on the team because of the high level of his offensive game. At that time, Allen was not merely restricted to shooting long jumpers. He was an all-around offensive talent that could score from anywhere on the floor. In his first season as a high school star, he averaged 18 points.

Because of the early skills that he displayed as a high school star, Ray Allen was already highly recruited even before his junior year in high school. His junior year became a turning point in his life. His girlfriend, Rosalind Ramsey, got pregnant. That made Ray-Ray think that his whole career path should be more focused on being able to play college basketball in a good school to get a top notch education. With that, he welcomed Tierra, his firstborn daughter to Rosalind.

Ray Allen worked on his basketball game in the hopes of landing a scholarship in a big basketball program. In the Nike Summer Camp before his senior year, Ray-Ray played against some of the best prep players the nation had to offer. Being around some of the best young guns in the whole country made Ray Allen think that he had what it took to get into the NBA after polishing his game in college. Some of his peers in the Nike Camp had that kind of a mentality. They were looking to get accepted into college to hone their skills in preparation for the NBA. But not everyone could get that far. Allen knew that, and he wanted to be the best out of the pack to make sure that his skills would be good enough for the big leagues.

Ray Allen's senior year in high school was the culmination of the basics he had learned since he was a child. After an early-season blunder that saw him making a tremendous dunk on his team's basket, Allen would never falter mentally again. His basketball intelligence was unparalleled for a young high school star, and it seemed like his smarts could take his team to new heights. Indeed, they did as Hillcrest would only lose four out of 30 games that season with Allen leading the way.

The team made it all the way to the state championship game. It was the school's first-ever chance at the state championship, and it was all thanks to the hard work and dedication that Ray Allen put into his game. Against Byrnes High School, Hillcrest was seemingly unstoppable as they opened up the game with a 26-point first half lead. Their opponents would rally back, but Allen took charge with his all-around game. He ended up with 25 points and 12 rebounds for Hillcrest High School on its way to winning the school's first state championship.

Chapter 3: College Career

Freshman Year

Ray Allen initially wanted to go to the University of Kentucky to join Coach Rick Pitino's squad. The Kentucky Wildcats were one of the most successful college programs in the whole nation. The school had won five national championships at that time and had been in the Final Four 10 times, including the year before Allen's college days began. However, Ray-Ray would join the University of Connecticut instead as he was banking on the promise of the coaching staff that the Huskies would be his team in no time. Assistant coach Karl Hobbs, the man that recruited Allen, really believed in what the young gunner could do as he was heavily courting him into going to UConn instead.

Though not as successful in basketball as Kentucky was, UConn was still one of the better college basketball programs in the country. But they've never been to the Final Four, let alone won an NCAA title. The farthest the school has been was the Elite Eight back in 1990. Allen was determined to change that. He wanted to bring a championship to UConn, and he was joining a squad that had all the makings of a deep run in the NCAA tournament especially with third-year forward and future NBA player Donyell Marshall leading the way.

Ray Allen, though he was not yet the star of the team, was nevertheless an integral part of the Huskies offense. With him chipping in with double-digit scoring numbers off the bench as the sixth man on the team, the Huskies were able to win their first eight games of the season. They started 1993-94 season 15-1. With a good record, they were tops in the Big East Conference, but could not win the Conference title. Still, they were a second-seeded team heading into March Madness. In his first season with UConn, Ray Allen averaged 12.6 points and 4.6 rebounds while shooting 51% from the floor as the best man off the bench.

The Huskies reached as far as the Sweet Sixteen in Allen's first year in college. In that round, they faced off against the Florida Gators, but were defeated due to crucial missed free throws by Donyell Marshall in the final stretches of the game. Despite that, UConn fans had a lot to cheer about because their freshman player off the bench turned out to be mature enough to become a big time player in the NCAA tournament. Allen was the team's second-leading scorer in March Madness though he was playing the role of a bench guy.[i]

Sophomore Year

When Donyell Marshall decided to try his hand at the NBA Draft before the 1994-95 season, Hobbs' promise to Ray Allen was fulfilled. He became a starter for the UConn Huskies in his second year in college. He not only began to start games, but also became the team's best player in only two years. That was also the year that Ray-Ray began to shoot more three-pointers. He reinvented himself as a deadly outside marksman for the University of Connecticut.

The Huskies were yet again a dominant team in the Big East that year. They were nearly unbeatable as a college basketball team, and they were ranked in the polls as the best squad in the whole country. UConn would go 30-2 in that season and was once again the top team in the Big East.

But, yet again, they would lose in the conference championships to Villanova, one of the two teams that were able to beat them all season long. That aside, Ray Allen's Huskies were once again the second seed in the NCAA tournament of 1995. Allen improved his numbers all around as he averaged 21.1 points, 6.8 rebounds, and 1.9 steals. He shot six three-pointers per game and was making almost half of those shots for an average of 44.5%. It was a stark improvement from his freshman year when he was just attempting over two outside jumpers and merely making one per game. He won the USA Basketball Male Athlete of the Year in his second season.

UConn made it as far as the Elite Eight in that season. They had only made it that far twice in the past and were looking to make history by breaking into the Final Four. For Allen's part, he was determined to be a part of school history. Ray-Ray lit up the UCLA Bruins for 36 points in that game, but he was a one-man team. In the end, UCLA got the victory despite an explosion for Ray Allen.

Third and Final Year

Ray Allen flirted with the idea of going professional after his postseason run in 1995. He could have been drafted as a top shooting guard in the 1995 NBA Draft, especially with how his other peers were not at the same level as he was when it came to outside shooting. Ray-Ray had an excellent chance of cracking the top 10 in the draft and may have even been drafted in the first five depending on the needs of the teams with the five highest draft picks. But Allen's family decided that it was best for him to stay one more year in college because even Ray-Ray himself believed that he still needed to polish up and improve his skills before making the jump to the NBA. It was a good decision on his part.

Ray Allen was in the midst of a rivalry with Georgetown sophomore phenom Allen Iverson. The rivalry was portrayed by the media as having started from their stint together as teammates in the World University Games in Japan. Iverson was a phenomenal scorer and was doing it despite barely standing 6-feet tall. But he was not as complete of a player as Ray Allen was. Allen was the complete package regarding his overall offensive capabilities. He could score from anywhere on the floor, but his outside shot remained his biggest weapon. That was something that his counterparts from the other teams did not have.

In that season, the Huskies weren't the lone dominant force in the Big East because the likes of Villanova and Georgetown were also fighting for the spot as the top team in the conference. In what was one of the most hyped battles in college basketball that year, UConn matched up against Georgetown. It was a fight between Ray Allen and Allen Iverson for not only conference supremacy but also for NBA draft positioning. However, Ray-Ray ended up losing that game to Iverson and Georgetown in a seemingly lopsided game. But Ray Allen took revenge in the conference tournament championship. The two schools fought in a tight game that saw Ray Allen hitting a clutch jumper in the end part of the battle to give UConn the victory and the Big East championship.

The Huskies won 30 out of 32 games yet again and even had a 23-game winning streak. Ray-Ray averaged 23.4

points, 6.5 rebounds, 3.3 assists, and 1.7 steals per game. His outside jump shot saw further improvement as he was making 3.3 three-pointers in 7 attempts per game. Allen was a consensus first-team All-American, the Big East Player of the Year, and the United Press International Player of the Year. The UConn Huskies were a top-seeded team heading into March Madness. However, the team would only make it as far as the top 32 in the NCAA tournament after losing to Mississippi State. As promised, Ray Allen only had to stay one more year and was on his way to the NBA Draft after his three-year run with the Huskies.[ii]

Chapter 4: Ray Allen's NBA Career

Getting Drafted

Ray Allen was entering a legendary draft class that would turn out to be one of the best in NBA history, and probably the best since the 1984 Draft. The 1996 Draft Class was in a league of its own with the likes of Allen Iverson, Ray Allen, Stephon Marbury, and Marcus Camby. Though Ray Allen had a stellar career with UConn and was a complete offensive package as far as shooting guards were concerned, he was not the projected top pick in the draft. His college rival, Allen Iverson, was the player that got the most attention because of his scoring prowess and because of his ability to break defenses down.

Nevertheless, Allen was entering the draft often compared to Michael Jordan for his offensive package. But, regarding shooting, Ray Allen was as pure as a shooter could be because of his quick release and his ability to come off screens to get wide-open looks at the basket. As such, he also evoked comparisons to Reggie Miller who, at that time, was leading the Indiana Pacers in scoring with his ability to hit quick jumpers. But many scouts thought Allen was a different kind of player compared to Miller. Ray-Ray was thought of as a natural scorer instead of a natural shooter because of the other aspects to his attack.

Ray Allen had good ball handling skills for a player that moved around so much without the ball. Something he had that most pure shooters did not have was his athletic ability. At 6'5", Ray-Ray had good size for the shooting guard position and was also very athletic. He could run the fast break at will because of his speed in the open court, and he could even finish strong at the basket. Despite all of those other offensive weapons that Ray Allen had, what impressed scouts and analysts alike most was his shooting. Allen had a penchant for finding screens and open spots on the floor, but he was not merely a spot-up shooter. Ray-Ray could create his shots off the dribble and could even pull-up from a distance if open.

However, Ray Allen was not the most coveted player in the draft because of a few weaknesses. For one, his dribbling skills were good, but were not at the level of a good NBA guard. Ray-Ray could not break defenses with his ball handling, unlike Allen Iverson. That was the first weakness he needed to resolve. Secondly, Allen was never a good passer. He knew how to make plays for his teammates, and he knew when to make the timely pass. But he just was not a player who could always make other players look good by only moving the ball around. Because of that, Ray-Ray did not have a lot of assists in college or even in high school. As such, he was a player you could never really trust to dominate the ball at every play. Other than that, Ray Allen's defense also needed work.

Despite a few weaknesses to his game, not a lot of shooting guards were initially on par with Ray Allen in the 1996 NBA Draft. Allen Iverson could play that position, but people primarily thought he was a point guard because he did not have the size to play the off guard position. Kerry Kittles did not have the clear shot that Ray-Ray had. And the 17-year old high school star Kobe Bryant was still so raw that his game needed a lot of work and polishing before he could even be compared to his other draft mates. Allen was as good as a shooting guard was supposed to be.

As the 1996 NBA Draft unfolded, Allen Iverson was selected as the first guard and as the top overall pick. He went to the Philadelphia 76ers and immediately produced as a young rookie. Wanting to get their hands on capable big men, the Toronto Raptors, and the Vancouver Grizzlies selected Marcus Camby and Shareef Abdur-Rahim respectively. For the fourth pick of the draft, the Milwaukee Bucks plucked Stephon Marbury out of Georgia Tech on the belief that he was the best pure point guard in the draft.

Wanting to pair a good point guard to their rising star named Kevin Garnett, the Minnesota Timberwolves offered a package to acquire Marbury. They wanted Marbury playing alongside Garnett because of his explosiveness from the point guard position and because the two players already had close ties back when they were in their respective prep years. The Timberwolves selected Ray Allen with the fifth overall pick but sent him and a future first-round pick to Milwaukee in exchange for Stephon Marbury. With the deal finalized, Ray-Ray was officially an NBA player and was set on moving to Milwaukee to join his first ever professional ball club.

Rookie Season

Ray Allen joined a Milwaukee Bucks team that rested on the high-scoring efforts of forwards Vin Baker and Glenn Robinson. As such, Allen was relegated to playing third fiddle to the pair of All-Star players. However, the two star forwards could only lead the Bucks to a record of 25 wins as against 57 losses in the previous season. Allen was in the middle of an identity crisis for the Milwaukee Bucks. Nobody knew if the team was trying to rebuild or if it was fighting for a playoff spot.

Nevertheless, Ray Allen was a starter for Bucks in an instant. In his first game, Ray-Ray hit two three-pointers for a total of 13 points. It seemed as though the Milwaukee Bucks had found a gem as Allen would score in double digits during the first three outings. All three of those games were technically blowout wins. Ray Allen would hit the 20-point mark three times in his first 20 games. The first was his third game, where he had 20 points. The other two were both 23-point games. The Bucks were 11-9 in that part of the season.

However, the Bucks would lose games in bunches from December 1996 up to January of 1997. While Allen would have good games in those stretches, the Bucks still played horrible to the dismay of the rookie shooting guard. The worst span of time for the Bucks was from February 21 to March 7. They lost eight straight games between those dates and it seemed as though they had lost all hopes of making it into the playoffs.

Despite the struggles, Ray Allen showed flashes of what he could be as a star player for the team. He scored his then career high of 32 points in a loss to Phoenix on March 25. By the tail end of the season, Ray-Ray scored more than 20 points in four of Milwaukee's final six games as the team constantly went to him to improve the rookie's confidence in preparation for the following season.

In his rookie year, Ray Allen averaged 13.4 points and four rebounds while shooting 39.3% from the three-point arc. He played barely 31 minutes per game and shot at least 11 field goals per game as he was merely the third option and third leading scorer behind Baker and Robinson. However, Ray-Ray was voted to the All-Rookie Second Team that year. The Bucks finished the season with a record of 33-49 and missed the playoffs.

Improvements

Ray Allen would improve by leaps and bounds in his second year in the NBA compared to his rookie season. By that time in his career, Allen was a designated go-to guy for the team after the Bucks had made an offseason trade that shook the roster. They traded their star big man Vin Baker over to the Seattle Supersonics and acquired two capable players. They received a capable and quick point guard named Terrell Brandon, and a big-time rebounder Tyrone Hill. Without Baker, Allen found himself more involved with the Bucks' offense.

Allen started the season off by scoring 29 on October 31, 1997. He shot 10 out of 20 from the field and also made 6 out of 9 three-pointers. He would score above 20 12 times in his first 20 games. That was a nine-game improvement compared to the pace he was at exactly a year before. Ray then broke out of the 30-point barrier in the 1997-98 season by scoring a new high of 35 points on December 20. It was in a 20-point blowout over the New York Knicks, and Allen also hit five three-pointers in that game. Allen's next 30-point game came in a win against the Houston Rockets on March 24, 1998. He had 33 points in that game while also chipping in 8 rebounds and five assists. His best game of the season was a tough two-point loss to the Minnesota Timberwolves in their final game of the regular season. Ray-Ray exploded for 40 points while shooting 15 out of 27 from the field and 6 out of 10 from the three-point line.

At the end of Ray Allen's second season in the NBA, his numbers had all improved across the board. He averaged 19.5 points, 4.9 rebounds, 4.3 assists, and 1.4 steals while playing more than 40 minutes per game. However, he was still awful from the field and his shooting clip was at 42.8%. His three-point marksmanship was also terrible as he merely shot 36.4%. Allen could only hit 1.6 three-pointers out of 4.5 attempts per game. Though Allen improved so much in his second season and though he was already the team's second leading scorer, the Bucks were still mediocre at best. They missed the postseason with a record of 36 wins as against 46 losses.

First Playoff Appearance

The NBA saw a lockout period in 1998 as there were labor disputes between the players' union and team owners. During that period, teams could not make roster decisions and could not even conduct training camps for their players. It was a period of stagnancy for most NBA players as they were not even allowed to use team facilities to hone their respective skills. When a collective bargaining agreement was struck between the two parties, the NBA season was able to start, but it was already February. Hence, the regular season was shortened to 50 games per team.

Before the lockout, the Milwaukee Bucks were still able to make moves to improve the team. The Bucks hired a new coach that went by the name of George Karl. Karl saw a successful stint with the Seattle Supersonics and was responsible for taking the team to the NBA Finals in 1996, only to ultimately lose to the powerhouse Chicago Bulls team. Furthermore, the team was also able to acquire another shooter named Dell Curry, who made his living by shooting the three-point basket at a high rate. Under Karl, the Bucks saw a more balanced offensive attack that still revolved around Glenn Robinson and Ray Allen.

Allen still continued to score well for the Milwaukee Bucks even as his minutes dropped considerably. In the shortened 50-game season, Allen did most of his scoring on double digits, but also broke out of the 20-point mark 13 times. He had one lone 30-point game in a win against the Miami Heat. Ray-Ray scored 31 points that night as he shot 11 out of 12 from the free throw stripe. Ray Allen averaged 17.1 points, 4.2 rebounds, 3.6 assists, and 1.1 steals while playing 34.4 minutes per game in his third season in the NBA. His field goal shooting improved to 45% while his free throw percentage increased to 90.3%. But his three-point accuracy was still nowhere near its peak. He shot only 35.6% in 4.2 attempts from downtown.

With George Karl at the helm of the Milwaukee Bucks, the team's winning percentage improved. They finished the 50-games season with a record of 28-22, thus winning more than half of their games for the first time in a very long while. Though Karl's coaching was the primary catalyst, Allen's improved maturity, alongside the acquisition of Sam Cassell and Tim Thomas near the tail end of the regular season, also played a prominent part in the Bucks' improvement. They were able to make the playoffs as the 7th seed in the Eastern Conference.

However, the Bucks would lose in the first round as the Indiana Pacers swept them in three games. In Ray Allen's first playoff series, he averaged 22.3 points on 53.2% shooting from the field and 47.4% from the three-point territory. In that round, Ray Allen was matched up with Reggie Miller, a player he had always been compared to. But, as history knows, the veteran Miller won out that matchup after torching Allen with two 30-point games in that series.

First All-Star Season

Ray Allen's hard work and dedication came to fruition during his fourth NBA season. At that time, he was already 24, an age where most basketball players mature regarding their skills on the hard floor, if not mentally. Much like in his college years, it did not take long until Ray-Ray would become the team's best player. In only his fourth NBA season, the Milwaukee Bucks was already his team. He owned the identity as the team's best player and go-to guy on the floor. The Bucks could only go as far as Ray Allen could take them.

Allen was not alone in the endeavor of carrying the Bucks. He had two All-Star caliber players joining him in that cause. First off was the high-scoring small forward Glenn Robinson, who was already one of the main guys on the team back when Allen was still playing for UConn. The other guy was Sam Cassell, a point guard with championship experience. Cassell was acquired in a trade that involved Terrell Brandon. He would provide the veteran smarts and championship experience that were needed at the playmaker position. Cassell handled George Karl's offense almost to perfection as that season was his best regarding assisting.

Ray Allen started the 1999-2000 season well and on fire. In just his first 20 games, Ray Allen had already made 34 three-pointers. In that regard, he was second only to Reggie

Miller, who had already hit 39 outside shots in his first 20 games that season. In that same timespan, Ray Allen had already delivered two games of scoring more than 30 points. In one of those games, he had 33 points and ten assists, but it was in an 18-point loss to Denver. Nevertheless, his team was still winning more than they were losing.

What made Ray Allen better that season was his consistency. In the past, he would have games of scoring more than 30 points, but would then drop down to low double digits in a few stretches of games. But in the 1999-2000 season, Allen was consistently scoring more than 20 points per game. In the 82 games that he played, he scored above 20 in 50 outings. He's only had nine games of scoring more than 30 points, but he made up for it with a lot of consistent shooting from the floor. It was also in that season when Ray Allen developed into a deadly NBA marksman from the outside after three years of struggling below 40% from that spot on the floor.

Because of his consistency and hot shooting, Ray Allen was nominated to his first ever All-Star game. In that match, he scored 14 points while playing only 17 minutes. Ray-Ray continued to play well after the All-Star break. By the end of the regular season, his scoring numbers, field goal percentage, and three-point percentage all shot up. He averaged a then career-best 22.1 points together with 4.4 rebounds, 3.8 assists, and 1.3 steals. He was the team's leading scorer. Ray Allen also shot then career-bests of 45.5% from the floor and 42.3% from downtown. He was attempting five three-pointers per game and was making 2.1 of them. Allen's 172 total three-pointers that season was second only to the 177 of Gary Payton. But he has already surpassed Reggie Miller in that regard as the veteran scorer managed to make 165 outside markers. Though Allen was second to Payton in three-pointers made, he was arguably more accurate. Payton attempted 520 shots from downtown while Allen only had 407 attempts.

With the Big Three of Allen, Robinson, and Cassell leading the way, the Milwaukee Bucks were once again a playoff team with a record of 42-40. They finished with the 8th seed in the East and were once again matched up with the Indiana Pacers in the first round of the postseason. It was once again Ray Allen versus Reggie Miller—a battle of the two best three-point shooters the NBA has seen in those days.

The two shooters battled it out in a tight Game 1. Allen scored 26 points while making two three-pointers while Miller delivered 21 markers. But it was Indiana that held on to a tight three-point win. Ray-Ray and the Bucks would even the series out in Game 2. Allen had 20, but he helped in limiting Miller to only 10 points. With Ray-Ray's help, the Bucks won Game 2 by 13. However, they would lose Game 3 by the same amount. In that game, Reggie Miller exploded for 34 points while shooting 4 out of 14 from beyond the arc. Though Allen would contribute 26, there was nothing he and the Bucks could do to stop the hot shooter from Indiana.

As the Bucks were merely one game away from elimination, they would yet again win a game by 13 points. In Game 4, Allen contributed 20 points to even up the series against the top-seeded Indiana Pacers. They were a gritty team, and they were not planning on going away that easy even though the Pacers were the favorites in that series. But, as we all know, all good things must come to an end. Reggie Miller made sure of that in Game 5 where he delivered 41 huge points to seal the fate of the Bucks. It was a tight game that saw Indiana winning by only one point. Had the Bucks stopped Reggie from scoring at least a point or two, the outcome could have been different. Nevertheless, it was still a good season for Ray Allen's first ever All-Star year. In that series against the Pacers, he averaged 22 points and 6.6 rebounds while shooting about 44% from the floor.

Getting Past the First Round, Conference Finals Appearance

The Milwaukee Bucks kept their roster and their core players intact for the 2000-01 season. With how the Eastern Conference was shaping up to be less competitive than the West, George Karl and his staff knew that they had a group of players that could take them far into the playoffs. Fortunately, the Bucks' Big Three, led by Ray Allen, would not disappoint their coach or their fan base on their quest to relevance in the postseason.

Ray Allen, in that season, proved that his first All-Star year was not a fluke. In the 2000-01 season, Allen was even better, and he arguably had the best season he'd had since coming to the NBA. He came out scoring at the start of the season, and he even had a 40-point outing. On November 11, 2000, Ray Allen shot 17 out of 21 from the field, 4 out of 7 from three-point territory, and 6 out of 6 from the foul stripe to score 40 big points. Unfortunately, the Bucks lost that game by 11 points.

Nevertheless, Ray Allen played with the same kind of consistency that made him an All-Star in the 1999-2000 season. Ray-Ray would score in double digits in all but one of his 82 games. He scored more than 20 points in 46 total games. Allen had 13 games of scoring more than 30, and three of those were 40-point games. On February 26, 2001, Allen scored 42 points including nine rebounds and 7 assists. He shot 6 out of 8 from the three-point line. He would establish a new high when he scored 43 in a blowout win against Utah in the middle of April. He shot 8 out of 14 from the arc. Because of his consistent shooting efforts,

Allen was an All-Star for the second straight season. He also won the three-point shootout in the All-Star Weekend.

At the end of the regular season games, Ray Allen averaged 22 points while establishing career-highs on rebounds, assists, and steals with 5.2, 4.6, and 1.5 respectively. He also shot new career-highs of 48% from the floor and 43.3% from three-point territory. His 202 three-point baskets were second only to Antoine Walker's 221. But Walker needed 603 shots to get there whereas Allen needed to attempt only 467. Needless to say, Ray Allen had already established himself as the best shooter in the league in that season. Aside from being an All-Star for the second straight year, Ray-Ray was named as a member of the All-NBA Third Team.

With a record of 52-30, the Milwaukee Bucks were the second seed in the Eastern Conference and were one of the most improved teams in the whole league. In the first round of the playoffs, the Bucks faced off against the Orlando Magic. They quickly defeated the Magic in four games by winning three. Allen averaged 24.5 points, 5.75

rebounds, and 2.5 steals in that series. It was their first playoff series win in a very long while.

In the second round, the Bucks met the tough and gritty Charlotte Hornets team. The Bucks won Game 1 easily with a 12-point game. Allen continued his excellent shooting ways as he had 26 in that first outing. He would score 28 while making four three-pointers in Game 2 to help his team escape a tight win and to go up 2-0 in the series. But the Hornets would rally.

Charlotte fought back on their home court to make the series closer after winning Game 3. Despite a double-double output by Allen in Game 4, the Hornets would still come out of that one as the victors as they tied the series two games apiece. The Hornets would again prove how much of a gritty team they were when they defeated the Bucks in Game 5 to take the series lead 3-2. In those three losses, Ray Allen shot awful from the field and was in a slump of sorts.

Ray-Ray broke out of his slump in Game 6 to force a final game in the series. He scored 23 points on 10 out of 19 from the field and 3 out of 6 from the arc. In the most crucial Game 7, Ray Allen went out to score 28 points on an efficient 10 out of 18 from the floor. With his help, the Milwaukee Bucks were able to force their way into the Conference Finals after holding back the tough Charlotte Hornets squad.

Ray Allen and the Milwaukee Bucks had a date with destiny in the Eastern Conference Finals. Ray-Ray would matchup against his old college rival Allen Iverson. At that time, Iverson had already been named the league's Most Valuable Player while also leading the NBA in scoring. He was a one-man wrecking crew for the Philadelphia 76ers who were also looking for a return to the NBA Finals. To have a chance of beating the 76ers, Allen would have to match Iverson point for point. He tried to do that in the first two games.

Ray-Ray scored 31 points on 12 out of 22 shooting and 4 out of 6 from downtown in Game 1. But Iverson had 34 to draw first blood in the series. Allen would take revenge in Game 2. The hot shooter scored 38 big points as he hit seven three-point shots to help his team steal home court away from Philadelphia. He also assisted in containing Iverson to merely 16 points in that game. Milwaukee would take control in Game 3 as they won it by six points. Allen had 20 in that game that Iverson missed.

With Iverson back in the lineup after an absence in Game 3, the 76ers would win Game 4 and tie the series up. Ray Allen was limited to just 14 points in a tight defensive contest. Though the Bucks would continue to play tough defense on Iverson in Game 5, they still could not stop Philly from winning it and taking the series lead.

With only one loss away from elimination, Ray Allen would go head-to-head with Allen Iverson in a phenomenal shootout in Game 6. Ray-Ray scored 41 points while making nine three-pointers. Meanwhile, AI had 46 big points to lead the Sixers. Unfortunately for Iverson, Allen had more help as the Bucks tied that series three wins apiece. But, in the most important game of the season for the Bucks, Ray Allen could not match the effort of Iverson, and they could not even stop him from doing what he wanted to do on the floor. AI scored 44 points while Ray-Ray had 26. With the help of Iverson, Philly went out to win that one by 17 points. With that loss, the Bucks were eliminated from a chance of going to the NBA Finals. Though disappointing, that season should have been a sign of better things to come for the Milwaukee Bucks and Ray Allen.

Back to Obscurity, Missing the Playoffs

Believing that their Big Three could still help the team back to the NBA Finals hunt, the Milwaukee Bucks kept their core of three scorers. For Allen's part, he started the season hungry for more. He scored more than 30 points in the team's first three games. In those three games, he shot a total of 16 out of 26 from the three-point arc. Ray-Ray led the Bucks to a 4-0 start in the 2001-02 season. They were 9-1 in the first ten games of the year.

Unfortunately, the Bucks would lose five straight games after their hot start. Allen was severely limited in his output in three of those five straight losses. The Bucks would trade wins and losses after that. Allen, however, would miss a few games at the end of December because of minor injuries. Those missed games cut his five-year perfect run in the NBA. Since getting drafted, he'd played in all of the

Bucks' games since 1996. When he returned in January, the team would go on an eight-game winning streak. Allen scored more than 30 in three of those eight games.

After that winning streak, the Milwaukee Bucks returned to a period of inconsistency where they would have short losing streaks to match their wins. Even though they were stuck in the middle of the pack, Ray Allen was named as an All-Star for the third straight season. Over a month after the All-Star break Allen missed a few games yet again due to minor injuries. When he returned in April, the Bucks went on a five-game skid at the time of the season where winning mattered most to get playoff positioning. The Bucks would break that streak in a game where Ray Allen scored a career-high of 47 points. He shot a high of 10 out of 14 from the three-point line in that game.

At the end of his third All-Star season, Ray Allen averaged 21.8 points, 4.5 rebounds, 3.9 assists, and 1.3 steals. He shot 46% from the field and 43.4% from the arc. He was an even better three-point marksman that season as he increased his outside attempts to 7.7 from 5.7 per game. Even after increasing his outside shots, his accuracy never faltered as he shot a new career high from that spot of the floor. Though Allen missed a total of 13 games in that season, he was the NBA's leading three-point shot maker with a total of 229 shots made. However, with a record of 41-41, the Bucks missed the playoffs for the first time in three years.

The Trade to the Seattle Supersonics

The Milwaukee Bucks kept Ray Allen and Sam Cassell on the team after a disastrous 2001-02 season that saw them missing the playoffs. They had earlier traded Glenn Robinson in exchange for Toni Kukoc and Leon Smith of the Atlanta Hawks. But many people thought that Allen's time in Milwaukee was up, especially with how the team was loving rising third-year shooter Michael Redd.

Allen would remain with Milwaukee for the majority of the season. He continued to play consistently, and he put up the same high numbers he'd always put up in the last five and a half seasons he'd played with the Bucks. As a Buck, he had four 30-point games all the while when Milwaukee was trading wins with losses. After playing 47 games with the Milwaukee Bucks that season, Ray Allen was dealt before the trade deadline to the Seattle Supersonics. In exchange, the Sonics had to part with their longtime franchise point guard Gary Payton together with capable wingman Desmond Mason. Ray Allen averaged 21.3 points, 4.6 rebounds, 3.5 assists, and 1.2 steals in the 47 games he played with the Bucks. His field goal shooting and his three-point percentage both decreased to 43.7% and 39.5% respectively.

Ray Allen joined a Seattle Supersonics team that was struggling to find its identity without their star guard, Gary Payton. Trading Payton meant that the team decided to go into a rebuilding stage. They thought that Ray Allen, at 27 years old at that time, was a good player to build on for the future. Allen made his Sonics debut on February 23, 2003. In a loss to the LA Clippers, he scored 26 points together with 13 rebounds, 9 assists, and three steals for a near triple-double effort. He did have his first triple-double that season in a 17-point win against the Los Angeles Lakers on February 28. He had 29 points, 10 rebounds, and 10 assists that game.

The game following his triple-double effort, Ray Allen scored 40 points in a win against the Clippers. With Allen in the lineup, the Sonics found themselves winning more games than they were losing. He was playing more than 40 minutes per game and was playing the role of an all-around player. Without any other piece to rely on other than Allen and rising versatile player Rashard Lewis, the sixth-year shooter was playing the role of a scorer, rebounder, and playmaker. By the end of the regular season, Ray Allen averaged 22.5 points, five rebounds, and 4.4 assists. In the 29 games that he played for Seattle, he had 24.5 points, 5.6 rebounds, and 5.9 assists. For the second straight season, Allen was the premier three-point shooter with 201 makes in 76 games. He was not an All-Star that year and the Sonics missed the playoffs in the ultra-competitive Western Conference.

All-Star Appearances and Missed Playoffs

With a core group composed of Ray Allen, Rashard Lewis, Brent Barry, and Vladimir Radmanović, the Seattle Supersonics were the deadliest three-point shooting team in the whole NBA. They led the league in three-point shots made and attempted while also being second in three-point percentage. Of course, it was all thanks to their best player Ray Allen. If you wanted a team focused on shooting long bombs, Ray-Ray was the man to get.

Allen continued to play the role of an all-around player with the Sonics. They were a team that relied on their star shooting guard to do everything. However, he did not play for the Sonics until late in December due to injuries. It was the first time since his rookie season that Ray Allen would miss a bunch of games due to injury. He would make his return on December 23 where the Sonics decimated the Phoenix Suns. Allen scored 24. In just his seventh game since coming back from injury, he had 42 big points after making 16 out of 27 from the field and 5 out of 12 from beyond the arc.

Allen would have his second 40-point game on January 24, 2004. He scored 41 in a win against the LA Clippers. Allen would continue to lead the Supersonics in scoring and almost everything else. Because of that, he was made his return to the All-Star game as the member of the Western Conference squad. After the break, Allen had his third game of scoring 40 or more points. He had 40 in an overtime loss against the Utah Jazz. He made 6 out of 11 from the three-point arc.

Ray Allen would continue to play like a star until the end of the regular season. In the 56 games that he played, Ray-Ray scored 20 or more points in 39 outings. He had eight games of scoring more than 30 while three of those were 40-point games. He averaged new career-highs of 23 points together, 5.1 rebounds, and 4.8 assists together with 1.3 steals. However, that season was marked with inconsistency and inefficiency as he shot only 44% from the floor and 39% from the three-point line. He made a total of 148 three-pointers though he could only appear in 56 games. Meanwhile, the Seattle Sonics could only win 37 games that season, and they missed the playoffs. It was Allen's third straight missed postseason.

The Seattle Supersonics, though having a mediocre 2003-04 season with their group of players, decided to retain the services of Ray Allen. They extended him to five more years with an $80 million contract. Ray-Ray would not disappoint the team, though he was locked in with a lucrative deal. He would lead the Sonics to a nine-game winning streak in the early part of November. In that streak, he had back-to-back 30 point games. He scored 34 against Memphis and then 37 in the next game in Philadelphia. He hit seven three-pointers against Philly.

With a healthy Ray Allen leading the way together with a much-improved Rashard Lewis, the Seattle Supersonics found new life and were turning into one of the better Western Conference squads. Though the team lived and died from the three-point line, they were still able to beat opponents because of their explosive offensive game. Because of the success that the team was seeing, Ray Allen was nominated to his fifth All-Star appearance. Meanwhile, Lewis saw his first ever All-Star game.

Allen would be more consistent as a scorer in his second full season with the Seattle Supersonics. At the tail end of the regular season, he had his first and only 40-point game against the New York Knicks. He hit 6 out of 11 three-pointers in that match. At the end of the season, Ray Allen averaged 23.9 points, 4.4 rebounds, and 3.7 assists. He had scored more than 20 points in 55 games. He had 19 games of 30 or more points. Though Ray-Ray was a more consistent scorer that season, his shooting efficiency dropped. Ray shot a career-low 42.8% from the field while his three-point shooting decreased to 37.6%. But even so, he was named as a member of the All-NBA Second Team.

Though Allen was facing one of his best seasons as a professional, what was more important was that the Seattle Supersonics were back in the playoffs with a record of 52-30. They were the third seed in a competitive Western environment. In the first round of the playoffs, the Sonics faced the Sacramento Kings. They easily handled their opponents in five games. In those five games, Ray Allen averaged 32.4 points. It was arguably one of his best performances in the playoffs. After scoring 33 in a Game 3 loss, Allen went on to score 45 in Game 4. He hit six long bombs in that game. In the closeout game, he had 30 points.

In the second round, the Seattle Supersonics ran up against the powerhouse San Antonio Spurs team. After playing only 13 minutes in Game 1, Ray Allen scored merely 8 points while his team lost that one by 22. Game 2 was not much different as the Spurs won that one by 17. Allen scored 25 in that game. Ray-Ray would have a horrible shooting night in Game 3. He went for 6 out of 23 from the floor while making merely 1 out of 8 from the three-point arc. Luckily, the Sonics escaped with a slim one-point win.

Ray Allen would have a bounce back game in Game 4. He scored 32 points on an efficient 12 out of 20 shooting. His efforts helped the Supersonics win that game by 12. With the win, Seattle tied San Antonio for two wins apiece heading into a pivotal Game 5. Back in Texas, the Spurs would take back the series lead by winning Game 5 by 13. Though Allen played particularly well in Game 6, the Spurs escaped that one with a two-point margin. That victory ended Allen's and the Sonics' return to the playoffs. After averaging over 32 in the first round, Ray Allen had a bit under 22 points in the six games he played in the series against the San Antonio Spurs.

Back to Struggles

After a successful season that saw the Seattle Supersonics making a good run in the NBA playoffs, Sonics head coach Nate McMillan decided to leave Seattle to take a bigger deal with the Portland Trailblazers. The man who replaced him was Bob Weiss. However, Weiss just could not replicate the same success that McMillan brought to the Supersonics despite keeping the same core that helped the team win 52 games in the regular season of the 2004-05 season.

At that period, the Sonics leaned on Ray Allen much more than they should have and much more than any team has ever had. The 30-year old Allen, who was already playing in his prime, opened the season scoring 31 and 32 in the first two games. In his first 20 games, he scored more than 30 points on five different occasions. Late in December, Ray scored 39 points in a win versus the Denver Nuggets. He hit 8 out of 14 three-point shots in that game. His season-high was a 42-point game scored against the Phoenix Suns in a double overtime victory. Once again, he hit eight three-pointers. For the third straight season and for the sixth time, Ray Allen was an All-Star.

As good as Ray-Ray was in that season, it was unfortunate that the Seattle Supersonics were not as successful as they were in the year before. They were losing more games than what they were winning. Playing in the Western

Conference meant that the Sonics were hard-pressed on landing a playoff spot. But even so, Allen continued to shoot and score well for his team. By the end of the season, Ray-Ray recorded a career-high in scoring. He averaged 25.1 points, 4.3 rebounds, 3.7 assists, and 1.3 steals. He improved to a 41.2% three-point shooting while making a career-high 3.4 three-pointers on 8.4 attempts. Ray Allen hit a grand total of 269 three-point shots, which was a new high for most three-pointers made in a single season. He broke a record previously held by Dennis Scott, who hit 267 three-pointers in the 1995-96 season. Also, in that season, Ray Allen moved up to the second spot on the list of most career three-pointers made. He was merely second to Reggie Miller in that regard. But, to his dismay, the Sonics missed the playoffs with a record of 35-47.

Final Season with the Sonics

Ray Allen's fourth full season with the Seattle Supersonics was more or less the same as his 2005-06 season. Without any other pieces to rely on in offense, the Sonics leaned heavily on the three-point shooting duo of Ray Allen and Rashard Lewis. In that season, Ray Allen was arguably at his peak regarding individual performance. In just his first 20 games, Ray-Ray had already scored more than 30 points on six different occasions.

On January 12, 2007, Ray Allen had the best single-game performance of his life. In an overtime classic versus the Utah Jazz, Ray Allen led his Supersonics to victor with a 54-poitn output. He delivered 8 out of 12 three-point shots and 17 out of 32 overall from the field. Just three games later, he would score 44 points in a loss versus the Denver Nuggets. He hit 6 out of 17 from the three-point line in that game. Just a game after that, he scored 36 in a win against the Minnesota Timberwolves. Ray-Ray was selected as an All-Star for the fourth straight season and for the seventh time overall.

But, the same as the previous season, the Seattle Supersonics would struggle a lot. Seeing as how the team was not going into the playoffs with the way things were going, Ray Allen decided to undergo surgery late in March 2007 to fix lingering issues on both of his ankles. In 55 games, he averaged 26.4 points, 4.5 rebounds, 4.1 assists, and 1.5 steals. The Sonics went 31-51 in that season and missed the playoffs yet again.

The Trade to the Celtics, Forming the New Boston Big Three, First NBA Championship

Because of their bad record in the 2006-07 season, the Seattle Supersonics won the second overall pick in the 2007 NBA Draft. They drafted future NBA superstar with that draft pick. However, instead of playing Durant with Allen and Lewis, the Sonics decided to start anew and rebuild with young pieces. They agreed to a sign and trade that sent Rashard Lewis to the Orlando Magic. Finally, they traded their superstar Ray Allen to the Boston Celtics in exchange for Wally Szczerbiak, Delonte West, and Jeff Green, who was the 5th overall pick in the 2007 Draft. The trade to the Celtics granted Ray Allen a chance to start anew and an opportunity to win an NBA championship.

After acquiring Allen, the Celtics were also able to acquire Kevin Garnett in a trade with the Minnesota Timberwolves. With Paul Pierce, Ray Allen, and Kevin Garnett in the fold, the Boston Celtics formed a new generation Big Three composed of three future Hall of Famers in their prime playing years. The trade rejuvenated the Celtics and made them into a powerhouse team in the NBA. In the offseason, the Celtics went on a European trip to strengthen the bonds of the team. During the trip, the trio was asked about who they think should get the last shot in a game-winning situation. Both Pierce and Garnett, who were clutch players in their own rights, said that the final shot should always go to Ray Allen. That was a testament to how great of a shooter and a clutch player Ray-Ray was even to superstars equal to his stature.

Ray Allen helped the Boston Celtics win their first eight games at the start of the season. In the team's second game when the Celtics defeated the Toronto Raptors in overtime, Ray Allen scored 33 points and reached the 17,000-point mark for his career. The Celtics were 18-2 overall in their first 20 games, and that included the 45-point destruction of the New York Knicks on November 29, 2007.

With Allen, Pierce, and Garnett leading the way, the Boston Celtics seemed unstoppable and unbeatable. Though Allen was used to being the first option in every team he'd been with ever since his second season in the NBA, he was playing third fiddle to Pierce and Garnett. But he did not mind because he was experiencing a team success he had never seen before. And though he was relegated to being the third option, he was still scoring well in the double digits. Initially, he was not selected to play in the All-Star game. However, after Caron Butler was slated to miss the midseason classic, Ray Allen was selected to be his replacement. It was his eighth All-Star game appearance and his fifth straight. Near the end of the season, Ray-Ray was reunited with his former Bucks teammate Sam Cassell, who was signed from free agency when he was waived by the Los Angeles Clippers.

At the end of the regular season, Ray Allen averaged 17.4 points, 3.7 rebounds, and 3.1 assists. His scoring average dropped by exactly nine points, but it was not because he slowed down as a player. It was simply because the Celtics had a lot of other weapons to choose from. Allen shot 39.8% from the three-point line and 44.5% from the field overall. He also shot 90.7% from the free throw stripe. It was the third straight season he shot over 90% from the foul line. With his help, the Boston Celtics completed one of the greatest single-season turnarounds in NBA history. They won 66 games, which was a 42-game improvement from the previous season. They were the best team in the whole league.

In the first round of the 2008 playoffs, the Boston Celtics faced off against the gritty and young Atlanta Hawks. In Game 1, Ray-Ray led the Celtics with his 18 points. He scored 15 points in Game 2 as they routed the Hawks once again. However, Atlanta fought back in Games 3 and 4. With Allen limited to merely 13 points, the Celtics lost by nine points in Game 3. Though the Celtics' star shooter would make five three-pointers for 21 points in Game 4, the Hawks held on to tie the series at two wins each.

Back in Boston, the Celtics returned to form after in beating the Hawks by 25 points. Allen had 19 points in that game. Unfortunately, Atlanta won Game 6 and put the historic Boston Celtics' season in jeopardy. But, in Game 7, it seemed like the Hawks had lost all gas. The Boston Celtics destroyed them by 34 points, and Allen did not even need to score big. He only had 7 points, but it was more than enough to take care of the tough Atlanta Hawks team.

In the second round, the Boston Celtics went on to fight off the Cleveland Cavaliers led by the transcendent superstar, LeBron James. In Game 1 of that matchup, Ray Allen did not score a single point. It was the first time in his career that he failed to score in the playoffs. Luckily, his team escaped with a tight four-point lead thanks to the 28 points of Kevin Garnett. Allen would chip in 16 points in Game 2 as the team blew the Cavs out of the Boston Garden.

Similar to the series against the Hawks, the Cavs protected their first two games at home. In Game 3, the Celtics could not stop the Cavaliers from imposing their will. In the end, Boston lost by 24 points. Though the loss was not as devastating in Game 4, the Celtics still lost by double digits. Allen combined for 26 points in those two games. He shot a combined 8 out of 22, including 2 out of 9 from the three-point line in those two losses.

Back in Boston, the Celtics escaped the Cavs with a seven-point win. Allen had 11 points in that game. He continued to struggle in Game 6. Ray-Ray scored only 9 points as the Cavs tied the series at three games apiece to force Game 7 in Boston. The bad shooting continued in Game 7. He shot 1 out of 6 for merely 4 points. Luckily, his output was not necessarily needed. LeBron James and Paul Pierce fought in an epic shootout. James scored 45 while Pierce had 41. Though LeBron won that one-on-one matchup, the Celtics escaped with a five-point victory to move up to the Eastern Conference Finals.

In the Conference Finals, they met the Detroit Pistons, who held the second best record in the NBA. For Allen, the shooting struggles continued. He scored only nine points on 3 out of 10 shooting from the field. But Boston escaped with the Game 1 win. Ray-Ray got out of the shooting slump in Game 2. He scored 25 points on 9 out of 16 shooting. But Detroit managed to steal that one away from Boston.

The Celtics would regain home-court advantage by winning Game 3 in Detroit. They ended up winning that one by 14 points while Allen also scored that many points. But Detroit fought back in Game 4 to win it by 19 points.

Ray-Ray returned to his poor shooting ways as he shot only 2 out of 8 from the floor. In the pivotal Game 5, the star hotshot scored 29 and hit 5 out of 6 from the three-point line. His output was necessary as the Boston Celtics won that one by merely four points. Allen continued to shoot well in Game 6 as he scored 17 points to help the team win the game and the series. After dispatching the Detroit Pistons in six games, Allen, Pierce, and Garnett were all heading into the NBA Finals for the very first time in their legendary careers.

The 2008 NBA Finals weren't going to be easy, though. The Boston Celtics, the franchise with the most NBA titles, were heading into a historic battle with the Los Angeles Lakers, the team with the second most championships, to relive the greatest team rivalry in all of basketball. Against Kobe Bryant, the 2008 league MVP, and a fellow 1996 draftee, Ray Allen was in a tight matchup as he would be tasked from time-to-time to defend against the league's best player. Luckily, he was not alone in that fight because the Boston Celtics had a lot of veterans like Eddie House, James Posey, and PJ Brown to help them in the fight.

In Game 1 of the historic 2008 NBA Finals, the Celtics rode a strong second half performance to give the team a 10-point victory. Garnett led them with 24 points and Allen chipped in with 19 points and two three-pointers. He also helped in limiting Bryant to 24 points. Ray-Ray would hit three long bombs in Game 2 to help the Celtics beat the Lakers once again despite a strong rally put on by their opponents in the fourth quarter. Allen top-scored for Boston in Game 3, scoring 25 points and hitting five three-pointers. However, the Lakers rode on the 36 points of Kobe Bryant to cut the series lead down to one.

However, the Celtics would take a commanding lead over the Lakers in a six-point victory in Game 4. In that game, Ray-Ray played all 48 minutes for the Boston Celtics as he displayed his superior conditioning. He scored 19 points in that match. Los Angeles would take Game 5 after holding off the Celtics up until the final minute of the game to extend the series to at least one more game. In Game 6, Ray Allen and the Celtics made history. Allen tied a Finals record of seven three-pointers to score 26 points to lead the Celtics. However, he was not the only player clicking in

Boston as the whole team erupted for 131 points. In the end, the Boston Celtics were just too hungry for the Lakers as they won that game by 39. By beating the Lakers in six games, the trio of Ray Allen, Kevin Garnett, and Paul Pierce, who was named the 2008 Finals MVP, won their very first NBA championship.

Failed Title Defense

In the 2008-09 NBA season, Ray Allen continued to play the role of Boston's designated outside gunner and its solid second option behind Paul Pierce. Because of how injuries sidelined Kevin Garnett in a bunch of games, the Boston Celtics could not replicate the phenomenal season they had in the previous year. Still, the team remained to be solid as one of the top squads in the Eastern Conference. They even started off with a 27-2 record, which was, at that time, the best regular season start in NBA history.

Allen looked as if he could not slow down even at the age of 33. At that age, most NBA players would move slower or would play limited minutes due to stamina and conditioning issues. But Allen was different. He was always well-conditioned as a player and always had the stamina of a gazelle. That allowed Ray-Ray to constantly move on the floor trying to find screens and open shots. With how well he kept his body in top form and with a better chemistry with Boston's other main players, Allen had a better season with the Celtics than the one he had in their championship run.

Though Ray-Ray was no longer the volume scorer he used to be, he would still have huge games for the Celtics. He helped the team win 19 straight games from November until December of 2008. In that stretch of games, he scored above 30 twice. He hit 6 out of 9 three-pointers against Indiana on December 3. On December 7, he made 7 three-point shots out of 9 attempts in another win against the Pacers. He had 35 points in that game. Ray Allen's season high was a 36-point output against the Toronto Raptors on January 11, 2009. In that game, he hit a season-high eight three-pointers.

For the second year in a row, Ray Allen was not initially considered an All-Star player despite his efforts in leading the Boston Celtics to one of the top spots in the East.

However, the Orlando Magic point guard Jameer Nelson was ruled out of the midseason classic. Allen was chosen to replace the injured All-Star playmaker. It was his ninth All-Star game appearance and his sixth straight. At the end of the season, he averaged 18.2 points and 3.5 rebounds while shooting 48% from the field and 40.9% from downtown. He also shot a career-high 95.2% from the foul stripe. The Boston Celtics were the second seed in the Eastern Conference with a record of 62-20.

In the first round of the postseason, Ray Allen and the Boston Celtics became part of one of the most exciting playoff series matchups in recent history. They went up against the younger and hungrier Chicago Bulls team led by Derrick Rose, the Rookie of the Year, and by sharpshooter Ben Gordon. Against the experience, talent, and veteran smarts of the Boston Celtics, the Bulls were still able to push the defending champions to the limit in that postseason meeting. However, despite missing their emotional leader and defensive anchor Kevin Garnett, the Celtics stayed strong against their younger opponents.

Ray-Ray struggled against the Bulls in the opening game of the series. In Game 1, he was limited to merely 4 points on 1 out of 12 shooting. He could not make a single three-pointer out of six tries from that range. As the Celtics struggled, the Bulls forced overtime on the strength of their star rookie Derrick Rose. Chicago ended up winning the extra period to take home court advantage away from the 2008 champs. But Allen fought back in Game 2 as he went up against Ben Gordon in a shooting exhibition. Allen hit six three-pointers for 30 points while Gordon had 42. The Celtics would take that close one thanks to a resurgent game by their star shooter. In Game 3, it seemed as though Boston had found their groove against the Bulls, who struggled to make shots. The Celtics won that one by 21.

Once again, the Chicago Bulls fought back hard. In Game 4, Chicago rallied in the fourth quarter to once again as they led the game by three with seconds to go. Ray-Ray, to the rescue, hit a three-pointer to send the game into overtime. He had 28 points in the match. Gordon hit his own trey in the extra period to force another five-minute extension. In the second overtime, age and exhaustion caught up with the Celtics as they never even had a chance to lead. In the end, the Bulls tied the series up two wins each. After a good Game 4 outing, Ray Allen would once again struggle. In Game 5, he was limited to 10 points, but Paul Pierce led a rally to tie the game up after trailing by double digits. The Celtics got the better of the Bulls in the overtime period as they won that one out to take the series lead once again.

Game 6 was the best out of the bunch. Neither team let up in the whole game. Even when the Celtics were up by eight points with two minutes left, Chicago ran back to tie the game. The trend went on and on until they had to decide the winners in a third overtime. On Allen's part, he refused to lose as he made shot after shot for a total of 51 points. He made nine three-pointers. However, despite a phenomenal performance from Ray-Ray, the Celtics could not beat the Bulls in the third five-minute extension. Luckily for them, the Bulls seemed gassed in Game 7 as the Celtics went on to win it by 10. Allen had 23 points in that closeout game.

In the second round of the playoffs, the Celtics were matched up with the Orlando Magic led by Dwight Howard. Ray Allen faced off against his old Seattle teammate Rashard Lewis. In the first game, Allen could only score 9 points as the Magic took the first lead of the series. It was a different scenario in Game 2 as the Celtics blew the Magic out with an 18-point victory. Ray-Ray scored 22 in that game. When the series shifted over to Orlando, the Magic would have their own blowout victory. They routed the Celtics with a 22-point margin. Allen scored only 8 in that game.

Ray-Ray would have back-to-back struggles in Games 4 and 5. He scored only 25 points in those two games and shot 9 out of 24. But, somehow, his team found a way to win back-to-back to take a 3-2 lead. With only one win to go, the Celtics were looking like they were going to the Conference Finals for the second straight season. But the Orlando Magic had something to say about that. Orlando won Game 6, a game wherein Ray-Ray could hit only two field goals and score only 5 points. In the do-or-die Game 7, the Magic ran away with a 19-point victory to advance to the third round and to eliminate the defending champions. Though Allen had a miserable series against the Magic, the Boston Celtics sorely missed the services of Kevin Garnett, who could have helped them to at least defend their title in the NBA Finals.

Return to the Finals

The Boston Celtics saw the return of Kevin Garnett in the 2009-10 season. The Big Three were reunited and back in full strength in their quest for another shot at the NBA title. However, it was during that season when the Big Three was turning into the Big Four. Starting point guard Rajon Rondo was turning into an outstanding player for the Boston Celtics, and his playmaking skills would help the trio of Pierce, Allen, and Garnett in finding and making easy shots.

With Garnett healthy and with Rondo emerging as a talented star, Allen's scoring numbers saw a dip in his third season with the Boston Celtics. Throughout the season, he would have only one game wherein he scored more than 30 points. Nevertheless, it was during that season when Allen hit an incredible milestone. He scored 18 points on

December 10, 2009 against the Washington Wizards. With those points, he broke into the 20,000-point mark in his total career points. However, Ray-Ray would not make it into the All-Star team for the first time in seven seasons. He averaged 16.3 points, 3.2 rebounds, and 2.6 assists while shooting 47.7% from the floor and 36.3% from downtown.

As Allen and the team continued to roll, the Celtics started the season 23-5. Despite the strong start, head coach Doc Rivers thought that his aging players could not keep up with the pace of playing heavy minutes night in and night out. He decided to limit the minutes of his Big Three. The decision hurt the team as they would go 27-27 after winning 23 of their first 28. Nevertheless, they qualified for the playoffs with a record of 50-32. They were the fourth seed in the Eastern Conference.

Though resting the stars seemed like a gamble that could have cost the Celtics home court in the first round, it looked like it paid off as the Boston stars seemed rejuvenated in the postseason. In the opening round, they easily handled Dwyane Wade and the Miami Heat in four games. Though Ray Allen started that series with an eight-point output, he scored in double digits in the next four games to average 17.8 points in the first round.

In the second round, the Boston Celtics completed an upset against the top-seeded Cleveland Cavaliers led by the two-time MVP LeBron James. In Game 1 of that series, Allen only had 14 points as LeBron muscled his way for 35 and the Cleveland victory. In Game 2, however, both Allen and the Celtics were clicking. Ray-Ray scored 22, and the team won that game by 18. In a quick turn of events, Allen once again struggled as he scored only 7 points in Game 3 that was won by the Cavs by 29 big points. But nobody thought that the Cavaliers would have nothing left in the tank in the remaining games.

As he usually did, Allen got out of the slump to score 18 in Game 4. He helped Boston win that game by 10 points. In a revenge game of their 29-point loss, the Boston Celtics torched the Cleveland Cavaliers with a 32-point victory in Game 5. Ray-Ray chipped in 25 in that game as they made LeBron look like he quit on his whole team. In Game 6, the Celtics survived a monster triple-double effort by James to win the game by nine points and the series in six games. Though it was not one of his better games, Allen's eight points were enough to help his team advance to the Conference Finals for the second time in three years.

In the East Finals, revenge was in the minds of the green squad as they faced the Orlando Magic in a rematch of the 2009 semi-finals showdown. This time, the Celtics had a healthy Kevin Garnett in the lineup and a much-improved Rajon Rondo running the show. Allen opened the series strong with a 25-point output to help his team draw first blood. He was limited to merely four points in Game 2, but his team escaped with a tight three-point margin. Game 3 was a different story as the Celtics won that one out by 23 points. Allen contributed to that effort with 14 points.

No team in NBA history has ever come back from a 0-3 deficit in a seven-game series to win it all. The Orlando Magic tried valiantly, but failed. Facing elimination and the 22 points of Ray Allen, Orlando escaped with a four-point victory. They then somehow made things interesting by winning Game 5 by 21 big points. Unfortunately for the Magic, the Celtics returned to form in Game 6. Allen scored 20 as they completed the series win over the Orlando Magic in six games. That victory assured them of a return to the NBA Finals and a chance to win it all for the second time in three years.

In a beautiful twist of fate, the Boston Celtics would meet the Los Angeles Lakers in the 2010 NBA Finals in a rematch of the 2008 edition. However, the Celtics were seen as the underdogs in that series as the Lakers were the most powerful group and were the defending NBA champions. The whole Celtic group had to bank on their veteran experiences to at least give the Lakers a run for their money.

In Game 1, the Lakers started like a house on fire. They scored relentlessly against the Celtic defense up until the end of the third quarter. Despite a valiant rally by Boston in the fourth quarter, LAL escaped that one with a 13-point win. Kobe had 30 while Allen scored only 12. But in Game 2, Ray Allen would make history. He made seven three-pointers in the first half alone to break Michael Jordan's Finals record of six three-pointers in the first half. After making another one in the second half, Allen became the only player in NBA history to have ever hit eight three-pointers in a Finals game. He finished that bout with 32 points and a victory for the green team.

After a historic night, Allen was quickly brought back to earth in Game 3. He could not hit a single field goal out of 13 tries as the Lakers won that game by seven points. The shooting woes continued for Ray Allen in Games 4 and 5. He scored 12 points in both of those games, and he could not hit his three-pointers. Allen went 0 for 8 in Games 4 and 5. Fortunately, the Celtics won both bouts to go ahead in the series 3-2. Though Boston was merely a game away from winning another title and the franchise's 19th overall, Laker head coach Phil Jackson, after the match, was not worried as he said that the Celtics' 3-2 lead was merely a function of the home-court setting in the Finals.

Back in Los Angeles for the last two games of the Finals, Jackson proved his statement right. The Lakers ran roughshod over the Boston Celtics in Game 6 for a 22-point victory. If the loss was not enough, the Celtics had to endure insult to injury when they lost their starting center Kendrick Perkins to a season-ending knee injury. That kept

Perkins out of Game 7, and it spelled doom for the Boston Celtics. Boston opened the final game of the championship series high. They finished the first half leading by six points in a defense-oriented matchup. In the second half, they went up by as much as 13 points as they led the Lakers 49 as against 36.

The Lakers rallied back to make it a 57-53 deficit by the start of the fourth quarter. But the task proved too difficult for the Celtics. The Lakers continued to rally until they gained control over the game in the dying seconds thanks to a three-pointer by Ron Artest. Allen, who had 13 points, cut that lead to three by draining his trey. But it was all elementary as the Lakers held on for an 83-79 victory to once again be crowned as the NBA champions.

The glaring statistic in that final game was rebounding. Los Angeles had 53 rebounds that included 23 on the offensive side. Meanwhile, Boston only had a total of 40 boards. They sorely missed the rebounding abilities of Perkins in that game. But that was not all. Allen, after scoring 32 points in Game 2, was practically invisible until Game 7. Nobody knows if it was the defense or his age that made

Ray-Ray struggle. All we know is that the Celtics could have needed more production from him and from the rest of their stars to win that championship. But hindsight does nothing. All that the Celtics could do was to build on that experience and come back in the next seasons stronger than ever.

Becoming the Best Three-Point Shooter in NBA History, Return to the All-Star Game

In the free agency period of 2010, a major power rift happened in the East as the Miami Heat signed LeBron James and Chris Bosh to team up with Dwyane Wade. With three top 10 players in their lineup, the Miami Heat were looking to put the whole league on notice and were also seeking to unseat the Boston Celtics as the new Eastern Conference kings. But Boston remained stable as Ray Allen chose to stay with the Celtics for two more seasons. He signed a contract extension worth $20 million in a span of two years. With his new contract, Allen would not disappoint the Boston Celtics as he played a more efficient brand of basketball in the 2010-11 season.

In a game against the Miami Heat on November 11, 2010, Ray Allen and the Boston Celtics defeated the newly formed Big Three of the East. Allen scored 35 points on seven out nine shooting from downtown. After that, Ray-Ray helped the Celtics win 14 straight games from November to December. With Allen playing well alongside Pierce and Garnett, it seemed like the Boston Celtics would not readily cede the Eastern Conference throne to the Miami Heat or any other up and coming team for that matter.

Ray Allen would once again make history in that season. On February 11, 2011 during a game against no less than the Los Angeles Lakers, Ray Allen hit three three-pointers to surpass Reggie Miller's record of most career three-pointers made. After Ray-Ray hit the record-breaking shot, Reggie Miller, who was on duty as a broadcaster in that game, stood up and congratulated Allen personally during a dead ball situation. It was a heartfelt congratulation from one three-point king to the next. There was no doubt that Ray Allen was the new greatest shooter in league history after erasing Miller's record.

In that season, Ray Allen saw a return to the All-Star game. It was his tenth appearance in the midseason classic, but it would become his last one. At the end of the season, Allen averaged 16.5 points, 3.4 rebounds, and 2.7 assists while shooting career-bests of 49.1% from the floor and 44.4% from beyond the arc. He helped the Boston Celtics win 56 games for the third seed in the Eastern Conference.

In the first round of the playoffs, the Boston Celtics faced the new and improved New York Knicks led by Carmelo Anthony and Amar'e Stoudemire. But the Celtics were hungry for another title run as they swept the Knicks out of the playoffs. Ray Allen averaged 22 points in that series. He shot 57% from the floor and 65% from beyond the arc. In Game 3, he had 32 points on 11 out of 18 from the floor and 8 out of 11 from the three-point line. The Boston Celtics, not only Allen, were looking like they were rolling towards another chance at the NBA crown.

In the second round, however, they would face the Miami Heat, who they defeated in the first round of the 2010 playoffs. The Celtics were also longtime tormentors of LeBron James, and the King was looking to get revenge over the team that eliminated him twice in the last three playoffs. It seemed he was on track as the Heat took Game 1 by nine points. Allen would play particularly well in that game as he made five three-pointers for 25 points. Unfortunately, Dwyane Wade was just unstoppable on his way to 38 points. The Celtics would also drop Game 2 to the Heat. In that game, LeBron had 35 while Ray-Ray struggled for seven points.

In Boston, the Celtics would get their lone win in the series as they took a blowout victory. Allen contributed with 15 points. Miami would take control and eventually win the series. The Heat won Game 4 by 8 and then Game 5 by 10. Allen scored 17 and 18 respectively in those games. It seemed that the younger and hungrier Miami Heat were just too much of a match for the Boston Celtics in that playoff series.

Final Season with the Boston Celtics

Shortly after the free agency period before the 2011-12 season, the NBA went into a lockout due to labor disputes. After a new CBA had been agreed upon by the team owners and the players' union, it was already December.

Teams were able to have short training camps as the season started on Christmas Day of 2011. In that opening game, Ray-Ray scored 20 points, but it was in a loss against the New York Knicks. He opened the new season well. However, Boston dropped the first three games of the season. In the first 20 games that Allen played for the Celtics, the team was 10-10.

The Celtics were trading wins with losses but were somehow winning more games. It seemed that age was catching up with them as they struggled in the compressed 66-game season. Allen struggled to put up points on the board as he was suffering minor injuries that saw him missing a total of 20 games. Nevertheless, he was still able to contribute well to the Celtics' cause as he averaged 14.2 points and 3.1 rebounds while shooting a new career-best 45.3% from the three-point arc. The Celtics were able to win 39 out of 66 games that year and were once again the fourth seed of the Eastern Conference heading into the playoffs.

In the first round of the postseason, the Celtics faced off against the Atlanta Hawks. Ray Allen missed the opening game, which the Celtics dropped to the Hawks. Boston took Game 2 in a tightly-contested action. Allen scored 13 points that night. He would once again miss a game. Fortunately, Boston was able to win Game 3. Game 4 was a different story as the Celtics took a 22-point victory against the hapless Hawks. Allen chipped in 12 points in his second game in the playoffs. In Game 5, the Hawks survived a one-point win due to a late-game blunder by Rajon Rondo. But the Celtics managed to lean on their Big Ticket Kevin Garnett in Game 6 to win it by three points.

The Boston Celtics would face the Philadelphia 76ers in the second round. The 76ers were also a young team. That meant that they were on pace to give the older Boston team a huge scare in the playoffs. Boston would survive Game 1 with the slimmest of margins thanks to a late game run. The Sixers would take Game 2 away with the second one-point win of the series. In the first two games of the series, Allen combined for 29 points.

The Celtics flexed their veteran muscles in Game 3, winning that bout by 16 points. Allen scored only three points for the green team in that match. In the second straight bad game for Ray-Ray, the 76ers would get another win as the two teams were merely trading wins with losses. In the third straight horrible game, Ray Allen scored only five points, but the Celtics took a 16-point win. Again, the Sixers were able to tie up the series with a win in Game 6. Luckily, Boston rode the cheers of their home crowd to survive a series scare from the eighth-seeded Philadelphia 76ers. Allen had 11 points in that game, and it was his only double-digit output against the Sixers.

In the Conference Finals, the Boston Celtics had one more chance to redeem themselves as they met the Miami Heat in a rematch of their 2011 second-round meeting. The Heat easily took Game 1 away with a 14-point win. Ray Allen continued to shoot horribly in that game. He broke out of the slump in Game 2, scoring 13 points on 5 out of 11 shooting. Allen shot the three-pointer that sent the game into overtime. But the Miami Heat took that one again, albeit in a tighter ball game.

Boston would make a run that started in Game 3. Back on their home court, the Celtics fed off the crowd to inch within one game closer in the series. Allen only had 10 points in that match, but he shot efficiently from the floor. Game 4 was another tight game. Boston was hitting their three-pointers, but the Heat fought back in the second half to make it a little more interesting. But Boston held on to win a tight contest by two points. Game 5 was an overtime thriller. The Miami Heat saw the return of Chris Bosh, who was injured in the previous round. The two teams fought in another tight game until the overtime period. The extra five minutes was a defensive dispute as the Heat could only score two points while the Celtics had four. Pierce made a three-point shot to give the Celtics the win.

With only one win to go before a return to the NBA Finals, the Boston Celtics could not stop the Heat from blowing them out in Game 6. They suffered the wrath of LeBron James, who had 45 points. With that win, the Heat sent the series into a do-or-die Game 7. In that game, the Celtics were still unable to stop LeBron from imposing his will. Though Boston started the first half well, they were winded in the second half as Miami went on to win the game by 13 points thanks to the 31 of James. After that devastating loss, it seemed as though that was Boston's final chance at an

NBA Finals spot. And, for Ray Allen, his days with the Celtics were numbered.

Joining the Miami Heat, Second NBA Title

Ray Allen's two-year contract with the Boston Celtics was up. When the Celtics offered him another two-year contract, which was worth $12 million, the 37-year old Ray Allen declined. He was already unhappy with the Boston Celtics. He did not have a good relationship with the Celtics' star point guard Rajon Rondo because of a short conversation they had in 2009. He was not happy with how the Celtics were treating him as an older player. Rivers had Allen coming off the bench a lot of times in the playoffs, and that did not sit well with him, especially with how he'd helped the team win so much. Years later, Paul Pierce would go on to say that they never felt Allen was really a part of the Big Three.

Sour relationships aside, Ray Allen took a pay cut to join the Miami Heat for a three-year deal worth a little over $3 million per year. He decided to go the way of joining the team that eliminated him twice in the postseason because the Heat were the defending champions and were in the best position to give him another title opportunity. As we'll see, it was a sound decision on the part of Ray Allen to join the team that had the best chance of winning an NBA title.

With the Heat in the 2012-13 season, Ray Allen came off the bench to spell minutes for Dwyane Wade and LeBron James. But he did not mind playing bench minutes because he was on a winning team. He was not the same high-scoring threat that he used to be, but he was still hitting timely shots and delivering clutch moments for the Miami Heat. His highest scoring output were 23-point games that he scored at the start of the season and the tail end of the regular games. In his first year in Miami, Allen averaged 10.9 points, his lowest since coming into the NBA. However, he was shooting 41.9% from the three-point range as an efficient outside gunner. He helped the Miami Heat win 66 games that included 27 straight, the second most in NBA history.

The Miami Heat marched along into the postseason as the best regular season team in the NBA. With the Heat, Allen found it much easier to score because of how much attention the trio of James, Wade, and Bosh were getting.

He scored 20 points in the opening game against his old team the Milwaukee Bucks in the first round. The Heat took Game 2 easily. In Games 3 and 4, Ray-Ray delivered 23 and 16 points respectively as the Miami Heat found him open over and over again. The Heat swept the Bucks in the opening round. In that round, Ray Allen surpassed Reggie Miller again. He broke Miller's record for most three-pointers made in the playoffs.

Miami would drop Game 1 of their second round meeting with the Chicago Bulls. But, in Game 2, Allen's 21 points off the bench helped the Miami Heat's 37-point victory over the Bulls. Though Allen struggled the rest of the series, the Heat didn't. Miami took Game 3 by 10. They then won Game 4 by 23. And, despite a tough fight from the Bulls in Game 5, Miami escaped the game with a three-point win. They defeated the Bulls in five games and were on their way to the Conference Finals for the third straight season.

Allen's struggles continued all the way to the Conference Finals series against the Indiana Pacers. He scored only four points in a slim one-point victory in Game 1. He had six points in a loss in Game 2 and then had the same amount of points in a blowout victory in Game 3. Ray Allen finally broke out in Game 4, but the Heat lost as the Pacers tied the series. Allen delivered seven points in an 11-point victory in Game 5, but would then score six in a blowout loss in Game 6. Finally, in the crucial Game 7, Ray-Ray contributed 10 points to help the Miami Heat win the game by 23. For the third time in his career, Ray Allen was back in the NBA Finals and was in a good position to win another ring.

Facing the San Antonio Spurs was not an easy task, especially since that team had not lost in the NBA Finals since 1999. However, the Miami Heat in the 2012-13 season was not an ordinary team. If there was a team that could beat the Spurs in the Finals, it was them. However, they would drop the opening game to the Spurs. Allen had a solid 13-point output, but it was for naught. He would again score 13 in Game 2, which was a huge 19-point win for the Miami Heat.

Game 3 was a different story. The Spurs were clicking on all cylinders as Danny Green and Gary Neal were hitting three-pointer after three-pointer. In the end, it was a no-contest as San Antonio took that one with a 36-point advantage. But Miami would take revenge in Game 4. Allen scored 14 points to help his team win the game by 16 and tie the series two wins each. Again, the Spurs were hitting their outside shots in Game 5, and Miami would lose that one by 10. Despite the loss, Ray Allen scored 21 points on a perfect 4 out of 4 from three-point range.

Game 6 was an instant classic for the Miami Heat. Playing at home, the Heat fought the Spurs hard thanks to the cheers of their home court fans. But the Spurs managed to hold a five-point lead with less than 30 seconds to go. Everyone in the building already thought that the Spurs had that one wrapped up. Miami fans were beginning to exit the building as the Larry O'Brien Trophy was already prepared for a possible presentation. But LeBron hit a three-pointer to cut the lead down to two points. The Heat fouled sophomore player Kawhi Leonard, who could only make one out of two free throws. In the next play, LeBron missed another three-point attempt, but Chris Bosh grabbed the offensive board and threw it into the right corner. In that corner, the player waiting for the ball was none other than Ray Allen. Ray-Ray hit a quick contested shot from that part of the floor to tie the game up with 5.4 seconds remaining. The Spurs would miss a possible game-winner, and the game went into overtime. Looking back, that was possibly the biggest shot of Ray Allen's career as he saved the whole Miami Heat season.

In the overtime period, LeBron hit a floater that gave the Heat a slim one-point lead. Ray Allen stole the ball away from Ginobili and was immediately fouled. With ice water flowing through his veins, Ray Allen hit the two clutch free throws to give the Heat the three-point victory. In Game 7, Miami rode the momentum of their Game 6 win to hold off the Spurs and to capture their second straight NBA title. Allen did not score in that game, but his season-saving efforts in Game 6 was more than enough contribution. As the buzzer sounded, Ray Allen was once again an NBA champion.

Back-to-Back Finals Trip, Final Season with the Heat

Ray Allen chose to stay with the Heat for at least one more season after he picked up his player option. He continued to play the role of sixth man for the Miami Heat in their quest for a three-peat. Ray Allen was still the best three-point shooting option for the Miami Heat that wanted to stretch the floor as much as possible. At 38 years old, he was in the twilight of his career, but his conditioning was still as good as that of a younger man. Allen was still quick when moving around the floor to find open spots. He was wearing the battle scars of a player in his 18th year in the NBA, but somehow, he was able to take care of his body to the point that he could still run with the younger guns of the NBA.

With Dwyane Wade missing a bunch of games due to injuries, Ray Allen was able to start nine games in the season, but coach Erik Spoelstra opted to play him off the bench for most games because he wanted the scoring punch that Ray-Ray could provide from the second unit. In his 18th year in the league, Allen averaged 9.6 points on

44.2% shooting and on a 37.5% clip from beyond the arc. The Heat won 54 games in that season on their way to the playoffs as the second seed in the East.

In the first round of the playoffs, the Miami Heat easily swept the Charlotte Bobcats. Allen was not much of a factor in that series because he only scored a total of 13 points in four games. He had no points in Game 1, and then only two in Game 2. He hit only 3 out of 13 from the three-point arc in that round.

In the second round against the Brooklyn Nets, Allen faced off against his old Celtics teammates Paul Pierce and Kevin Garnett. As if he wanted to prove something to his old running mates, Allen came out to score 21 points in Game 1 of the series. He hit 4 out of 7 from the three-point arc. His Game 1 performance against Brooklyn was already more than what he contributed in four games against the Bobcats. He would again play well in Game 2 as he scored 13. With his help, the Heat were up 2-0 against the team they could not beat in four games during the regular season.

Allen would slow down in Game 3 as he only scored 9 points in a Brooklyn win. But, he immediately went back to work in Games 4 and 5. He scored 11 and 13 in those respective games all the while when the Heat was beating the Nets in five games. After destroying the Brooklyn Nets, the Miami Heat were on their way to their fourth straight Conference Finals appearance. Ray Allen, after scoring merely 13 points in the first round, averaged 13 points against Brooklyn.

The Miami Heat faced the Indiana Pacers in a rematch of the 2013 Eastern Conference Finals. Indiana took Game 1 with an 11-point victory. Allen had 12 in that game. But the Heat would go on to win three straight games. In Game 2, Allen could only score three points. He bounced back in Game 3 where he delivered 16 points on a perfect 4 out of 4 from the three-point line. Ray-Ray had 9 in Game 4. Though Allen would score 15 in Game 5, the Pacers took that close one to get closer to Miami in the series. But that was the closest they could get as the Heat closed them out in Game 6 with a 25-point rout. Ray Allen was on his way to his fourth NBA Finals appearance.

In the 2014 NBA Finals, the Miami Heat had to once again try to beat the San Antonio Spurs for basketball immortality. But the 2014 edition of the Spurs were different from their 2013 counterparts. They were hungrier and were playing out of their minds. Their ball movement was the best it ever was, and they were easily blowing out their opponents in the playoffs. It seemed like the road to a three-peat was not going to be an easy one for the Miami Heat.

The San Antonio Spurs started Game 1 like a house on fire. They shot three-pointers after three-pointers while also pouring in timely shots inside the paint. The Heat seemed helpless as they lost that one by 15. Allen would score 16 points in that game, but that was his best for the series. The Heat would play the Spurs tight in Game 2. Thanks to a timely three-point shot by Chris Bosh in the end game, Miami was able to take one away from the Spurs. However, things went downhill from there.

The Spurs totally decimated the Miami Heat from Game 3 onwards. They were moving the ball at such a speed that the Heat defenders could not keep up. At the end of the third game, the Spurs were up 19. Game 4 was more of the same. All the Spurs players were clicking like nobody could stop them from putting points on the score sheet. San Antonio took that one by 21 points. In the fifth game, LeBron pleaded with his team to follow his lead. However, the Spurs were just too good that season. San Antonio destroyed the Miami Heat's chances at a three-peat by defeating them in Game 5 by 17 points. With that loss, the Miami Heat were sent home packing and contemplating the long summer ahead of them. Their Big Three had the option to opt out of the contract while Ray Allen could actually already retire.

Sitting Out, No Official Retirement

As it turned out, the 2013-14 season was Ray Allen's final one with the Miami Heat. He became a free agent shortly after losing to the San Antonio Spurs in the 2014 NBA Finals. Initially, no team wanted to sign the services of the hotshot during the free agency fever in the offseason before the 2014-15 season. Eventually, the season started with Allen still jobless.

After long contemplation and deliberation, Ray Allen, at 39 years old, announced that he would sit out the entire 2014-15 season even with numerous teams interested in him. The new and improved Cavaliers team with James, Irving, and Love wanted to sign him.[iii] Even the historical 2014-15 edition of the Golden State Warriors were interested in adding one more all-time shooter to their lineup. In the end, Allen decided not to take up any offers as he wanted to assess his situation first and spend time with his family.[iv] It was such a shame that he had to take a long vacation because a lot of NBA teams could have used his services from the outside. Had he signed with LeBron and the Cavaliers, he could have made a difference in the NBA Finals of 2015. Had he signed with the Warriors, Ray Allen could very well be a three-time champion already.

Even in the 2015-16 season, Ray Allen remains without a team. At 40 years old, he would become the oldest player in the NBA if ever he gets signed into a team. Even at that age, Ray-Ray continued to work out and to keep his body in shape for a possible quick job with an NBA team. He still has not announced an official retirement, and he has not even contemplated doing so.[v] With plenty left in the tank, Ray Allen may see a return to the NBA floor to do what he does best—shoot the three-ball.

Chapter 5: Ray Allen's Personal Life

Ray Allen's father is Walter Allen, Sr. The elder Allen worked as a welding specialist with the military during Ray-Ray's younger years. As such, he and his family frequently moved from one base to another. Ray's mother is Flora Allen. Flora was always a big fan of her son. She was often seen watching Ray-Ray's home games, especially when her son moved over to Boston.

Ray Allen is the middle child of five siblings. He has three sisters and one brother. His sisters are Talisha, Kim, and Kristie, while his brother's name is John. Ray is married to Shannon Walker Williams, who he married in August of 2008 after dating for four years. Williams works as an actress and as a singer. Together, they have three children named Tierra, Ray III, and Walker. Ray's second son Walker suffers from Type 1 Diabetes.

Allen has appeared in the film "He Got Game", which was produced by longtime NBA fan Spike Lee in 1998. He starred together with Denzel Washington and played the role of a high school basketball superstar named Jesus

Shuttlesworth. He also appeared in a film called "Harvard Man", which was released in 2001. Ray Allen played the role of Marcus Blake.

Chapter 6: Ray Allen's Legacy and Future

There is no doubt in anyone's mind that Ray Allen is one of the best shooters in the long history of the NBA. The NBA has seen an extensive list of great shooters such as Jerry West, Larry Bird, Dell Curry, Reggie Miller, Drazen Petrovic, Peja Stojakovic, Steve Nash, and many more. But Ray Allen has either surpassed or outlasted all of those shooters on his way to becoming the player that converted the most three-point shots in the history of the NBA. While shooting is first and foremost a talent, the only way to hone it is through practice and a lot of repetition. It is said that Allen shoots about 200 three-pointers per hour during his training days. Aside from that, Allen was able to last long in the NBA because he worked on his conditioning. That allowed him to run tirelessly around the court to look for screens and open spots on the floor. He has one of the best conditioning regimens in the entire NBA, and that helped him play beyond his years.

While Allen is known primarily for his three-point shooting, he is not a one-dimensional player. Throughout his 18-year career, Ray Allen has scored 18.9 points per game for a total of 24,505. In that same span, he has made and attempted 2.3 three-pointers out of 5.7. If all that Allen did was shoot three-point shots, then he should not have scored over 24,000 points. In his younger years, Allen was a complete scorer. He could drive and finish strong at the basket while also making perimeter shots off the dribble. With a total of 4,398 free throws out of 4,920, Ray Allen was also gifted in drawing fouls. Given his vast array of offensive moves, Ray-Ray was anything but a one-dimensional scorer.

As far as shooters go in the history of the NBA today, nobody has made more three-point shots than Ray Allen. With a career total of 2,973 three-pointers, nobody is even close to him in that regard. He's hit over 400 more outside shots than Reggie Miller has, and over 800 more than Jason Terry, the third guy on the list. Because of his total three-point shots made, Ray Allen is widely regarded as the best shooter in NBA history. While there are players today who are on track of beating his record, Allen's longevity and success in an 18-year career remain unmatched for those shooters.

As a member of the Milwaukee Bucks, Ray Allen is arguably the best shooter in the franchise's history. Nobody in a Bucks uniform has ever made more three-point shots than Ray Allen. While Allen was replaced by Michael Redd as Milwaukee's hotshot from the outside, Redd never replicated the same success that Allen has had team-wise. Ray-Ray, with 1,051 three-pointers, has made the most three-point field goals in Milwaukee history. He's also fourth on the franchise's list of career scorers.

When you look at the list of most three-point field goals made in Seattle Supersonics or Oklahoma City Thunder history, Ray Allen is fourth on that list. Kevin Durant, Rashard Lewis, and Gary Payton have made more than he did while playing for the Sonics and Thunder. However, Allen has only played for the Sonics for four and a half seasons. All three players above him on the list have played a lot more seasons with the Sonics and Thunder franchises than he ever did. Considering that Allen needed only four and a half seasons to get to 869 three-pointers whereas Kevin Durant needed seven to get to that number, you cannot discount the fact that Ray Allen is the Sonics' and Thunder's most prominent three-point shooter.

Though Ray Allen was past his prime years when he played for the Boston Celtics and the Miami Heat, it cannot be ignored that he still contributed a lot for both franchises because of his shooting. As a Celtic, he was the third member of the new era's Boston Big Three that won a title in 2008. He was the designated outside threat for that team, and he's bailed them out of tight situations just by shooting the three-pointer. As a member of the Heat, Allen was 38 years old and was at an age where he could not set records anymore. But who could ever forget that clutch three-pointer he made in Game 6 of the 2013 NBA Finals. That shot saved the Heat's season and helped them win the franchise's third NBA Championship.

In his long career, Ray Allen has averaged 18.9 points, 4.1 rebounds, 3.4 assists, and 1.1 steals. He's made 45.2% of all of his shots and 40% of his three-pointers. Ray Allen has become an All-Star 10 times and an All-NBA Team member twice. He's won the NBA championship twice (once as a Celtic and once with the Heat). He has also won the Three-Point Shootout once in his career. Allen helped revolutionize an NBA that has trended towards more three-point shooting than it ever has since the inception of the three-point arc in the 1979-80 NBA season.

Because of Ray Allen's volume three-point shooting, a lot of NBA players today have trended towards specializing in that department. Make no mistake. There have been a lot of past NBA players that lived and died in the three-point line. However, what makes today's generation of shooters different is that they not only make the outside shot at a high rate but they also score a lot of points other than from the three-point line much like Ray Allen did. Today, you have the likes of Stephen Curry, Klay Thompson, Kevin Durant, Damian Lillard, Kyle Korver, and James Harden. All of those players have made the three-pointer their specialty. However, they have also been All-Star players not because of their shooting, but because of their all-around scoring abilities. It's safe to say that they have followed the footsteps of Ray Allen as perennial scorers who shoot the outside shot at high clips.

While we may see some of those players breaking Allen's three-point record someday, it cannot be denied that Allen provided inspiration for those younger players. Without him, young shooters would have never had the guts to become volume shooters from the outside. Today, both Curry and Thompson together with Harden and Lillard are on pace to making more career three-pointers than Ray Allen in his 18 years in the NBA. Barring injury, we may see three or four players from today's generation making more career three-point shots than Ray Allen. That's how much the NBA has changed, and that's how much today's players have all been inspired to shoot a lot more three-balls than any other generation has.

Steph Curry, who owns the top three three-point shooting seasons in NBA history, is the top contender for Allen's crown as the best shooter in league history. In just seven seasons, he's already halfway to breaking Ray-Ray's career three-point shooting record. He's been making 3.1 three-pointers per game whereas Allen's made 2.3. Many have already been calling Curry the best shooter in NBA history because of his incredible shooting display since 2014. Though he may have already surpassed Allen in skill, and would soon break the three-point shooting record, there can be no denying how much Ray-Ray has done for the sport of basketball because of his ability to shoot. He may not already be the best at what he does, but Ray Allen will always stay as one of the finest shooters to have ever graced the NBA hard floor. If we might not remember him holding the NBA record for most three-pointers made in a career, we'll always remember the dozens of clutch shots and buzzer-beating long bombs he's made in his long NBA years.

Final Word/About the Author

I was born and raised in Norwalk, Connecticut. Growing up, I could often be found spending many nights watching basketball, soccer, and football matches with my father in the family living room. I love sports and everything that sports can embody. I believe that sports are one of most genuine forms of competition, heart, and determination. I write my works to learn more about influential athletes in the hopes that from my writing, you the reader can walk away inspired to put in an equal if not greater amount of hard work and perseverance to pursue your goals. If you enjoyed *Ray Allen: The inspiring Story of One of Basketball's Greatest Shooters,* please leave a review! Also, you can read more of my works on *Colin Kaepernick, Aaron Rodgers, Peyton Manning, Tom Brady, Russell Wilson, Michael Jordan, LeBron James, Kyrie Irving, Klay Thompson, Stephen Curry, Kevin Durant, Russell Westbrook, Anthony Davis, Chris Paul, Blake Griffin, Kobe Bryant, Joakim Noah, Scottie Pippen, Carmelo Anthony, Kevin Love, Grant Hill, Tracy McGrady, Vince Carter, Patrick Ewing, Karl Malone,*

Tony Parker, Allen Iverson, Hakeem Olajuwon, Reggie Miller, Michael Carter-Williams, John Wall, James Harden, Tim Duncan, Steve Nash, Pau Gasol, Marc Gasol, Jimmy Butler, Dirk Nowitzki, Draymond Green, Pete Maravich and Kawhi Leonard in the Kindle Store. If you love basketball, check out my website at claytongeoffreys.com to join my exclusive list where I let you know about my latest books and give you lots of goodies.

Like what you read? Please leave a review!

I write because I love sharing the stories of influential people like Ray Allen with fantastic readers like you. My readers inspire me to write more so please do not hesitate to let me know what you thought by leaving a review! If you love books on life, basketball, or productivity, check out my website at claytongeoffreys.com to join my exclusive list where I let you know about my latest books. Aside from being the first to hear about my latest releases, you can also download a free copy of *33 Life Lessons: Success Principles, Career Advice & Habits of Successful People*. See you there!

Clayton

References

[i] "Ray Allen". *JockBio.* Web

[ii] "Ray Allen". *JockBio.* Web

[iii] Harper, Zach. "Report: Ray Allen will play in 2014-15, Cavaliers are frontrunners". *CBS Sports*. 9 August 2014. Web

[iv] d'Oliveira, Sean. "Ray Allen announces decision to sit out the 2014-15 season". *CBS Sports*. 4 March 2015. Web

[v] Pandian, Ananth. "After taking season off, Ray Allen, 40, says he 'won't officially retire' yet". *CBS Sports*. 3 August 2015. Web

16878121R00064

Made in the USA
San Bernardino, CA
20 December 2018